Laugh Your Way to Happiness
101 Ways to
Have a Great Laugh

By Karith Foster

America's Girlfriend

Laugh Your Way to Happiness
101 Ways to Have a Great Laugh

First Edition

ISBN: 978-0-578-08070-3

Printed in U.S.A. by Instantpublisher.com

Cover Photo Courtesy of Mindy Tucker www.withreservation.com

Cover Design by Nancy Kekich

Edited by Carol D. Foster

Dedicated to my incredibly hysterical family: Queen Mum and Daddy, my brother DeWitt, “Gramcracker” and Grandma “V” whose conversations always cracked me up, and to ALL of my friends who’ve made me laugh so hard I’ve cried.

Thank you all.

Foreword

So, you're actually reading the foreword? Who reads the foreword? Now you're wondering, "Why is Saranne Rothberg (me) entrusted with the forward to Karith's "Laugh Your Way to Happiness: 101 Ways to Have a Great Laugh?" Actually, Karith had no choice; I have some pretty incriminating photos of your author, "America's Girlfriend". Just kidding.

CNN, Oprah, The NY Times call me a "Happiness and Laughter Expert" because when I was diagnosed with stage 4 cancer in 1999 I threw a "Chemo Comedy Party" from my chemo chair during my first treatment and then invited the other patients and caregivers to laugh and celebrate with me; that night I launched www.ComedyCure.org® armed with the notion that "laughter is the best medicine." I refused to let cancer rob my Laughter and abscond with my Happiness. Over the past decade, I have helped almost 700,000 kids and adults living with stress, trauma and illness rediscover their funny bones through our live ComedyCures® events. Karith and I met at the beginning of her comedy career when she volunteered her talent for a ComedyCures® patient event. We forged a great friendship and Karith and I have reunited on ComedyCures® stages at the United Nations, hospitals and many major comedy clubs.

Karith has gone onto become a successful TV/Radio Host, Actress, National Speaker and Author. Working with ComedyCures® was a big part of Karith's inspiration for writing this book. It is the perfect "pick-me-up" when you feel blue- you can use her many fun suggestions as great icebreakers for any party or just give the whole book as a fun gift.

Karith (and you too) will be supporting free ComedyCures® programs for patients because Karith is donating a portion of the proceeds from every book to our award-winning non-profit organization. Now, your laughter can be contagious too. We get very good at what we practice- Karith is showing us all how to practice more Happiness and to increase the Laughter in our daily life. Enjoy!

Saranne Rothberg

CEO, The ComedyCures Foundation®

www.ComedyCures.org

Introduction:

e.e. cummings said it best when he wrote, "The most wasted of all days is one without laughter." I couldn't agree more; not just because I'd be out of a job as a comedian, but because laughter is one of the best antidotes to anything negative. Laughter is cathartic; it is healing; it promotes bonding; it can lighten almost any tense situation and brighten the darkest of moods.

Numerous studies that have been conducted on laughter show that children laugh way more than their adult counterparts. So, where did the laughter go? Well, that answer is simple. When we grew up so did our problems and responsibilities. But just because we're no longer kids doesn't mean we shouldn't still smile, have fun and laugh regularly.

That is the purpose of this fun little book. To remind you that having a great laugh is easier than thought and often cheaper than Prozac. No doubt, the key to increasing joy and happiness in your life lies in how much laughter you experience.

The ability to laugh at yourself and the world around you is a gift. So what are you waiting for? It's time to take back your happiness and bring more joy into your life. Laughter is your birthright, a natural part of life that is innate and inborn. So read this book, follow the instructions and have a GREAT Laugh!

~Karith

1. Go to the park and watch kids play- not in a creepy making parents so-uncomfortable they-want-to-call-the-cops-way. Just hang; observe how easily children interact and enjoy their imagination. They crack themselves & each other up.

2. Rent, buy or download a season of *Will & Grace, Friends* or *Seinfeld.* Then watch it!

Laughter Exercise

Write down 5 of your favorite episodes or lines from *Will & Grace, Friends* or *Seinfeld*:

1.________________________

2.________________________

3.________________________

4.________________________

5.________________________

3. Look at old pictures from Halloween.

4. Go to a comedy club to see professional funny people on a weekend.

5. People watch @ the airport.

6. Skype™ or call up your best friend- the one who makes you laugh so hard you cry.

I am thankful for laughter, except when milk comes out of my nose.

-Woody Allen

7. Go rollerblading- especially if you never have before. (Author's note: please be sure to have all your gear on properly. Flesh wounds and broken bones aren't funny I don't care what Wyle E. Coyote does.)

8. Watch squirrels and watch them watching you.

9. Go to an amusement park or carnival.

10. Tell your favorite joke to someone. Sometimes that alone will crack YOU up.

Laughter Exercise

Write out your favorite joke:

____

____

____

____

____

____

11. Play with a puppy.

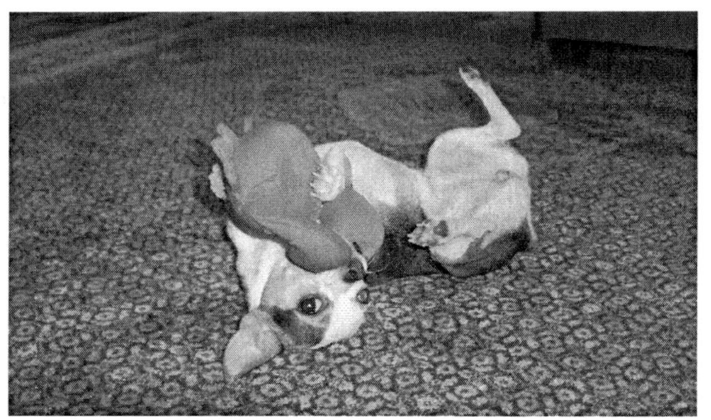

12. Watch a countdown or commentary show on TV where comics get to share their humorous two cents.

13. Buy a CD or download the stand-up comedy routine of one of your favorite comedians. Listen to it in the car or on your commute to work. I hear Karith Foster's "Straight Outta Plano" CD is the bomb!

What soap is to the body,
laughter is to the soul.

-Yiddish Proverb

14. Visit a toy store- like FAO Schwartz- but don't just be an observer; log some time playing with the toys.

15. Check out the humor section on the website www.HuffingtonPost.com

16. Go camping! Nothing brings out the funny like Mother Nature. If you're not a "camper" go camping just so you have the cocktail story.

17. YouTube™: laughing babies

18. Rent, buy or download the movie "Airplane".

Laughter Exercise

Write down 5 of your favorite lines or scenes from the movie "Airplane":

1. ______________________________

2. ______________________________

3. ______________________________

4. ______________________________

5. ______________________________

19. People watch @ the beach.

20. Buy a joke book. Then read it (Duh!)

21. Play a round of miniature golf with friends.

22. Go to or host a costume party.

Dogs laugh, but they laugh with their tails. What puts man in a higher state of evolution is that he has got his laugh on the right end.

-Max Eastman

23. Volunteer to take kids on an outing. Doesn't matter if they're children you know or if you're volunteering for a good cause. Listen to them-- you'll love what you hear.

24. Watch cartoons.

25. Rent, buy or download the movie "Shrek". (If that doesn't make you laugh a little or at least smile I can't help you.)

Laughter Exercise

Write down 5 of your favorite lines or scenes from the movie "Shrek":

1. ______________________________

2. ______________________________

3. ______________________________

4. ______________________________

5. ______________________________

26. Take your inner child on a trip to the zoo. You know a stop by the monkey cage is a MUST!!!

27. Have friends over for a board game night. Who does that anymore? It'll be a blast!

28. YouTube™: kitten slap

29. Go on a blind date (ONLY if you're single) even if you don't laugh on the date you'll have something funny to tell your friends afterward- especially if it was awful.

Even if there is nothing to laugh about, laugh on credit.

-Author Unknown

30. Get a picture taken with someone in a costume- theme parks are great for this, but you could even stop when you see a guy dressed as Uncle Sam or a woman dressed in a Lady Liberty costume advertising for a place that does your taxes.

STAR
1

31. Look at old family photos-Olan Mills portraits are always classic.

32. If by chance you don't have your own funny family portraits a) that's a shame and b) you should definitely visit: www.awkwardfamilyphotos.com

33. Play Twister (But only with people who you know use deodorant. ☺)

34. Watch monologues from the late night talk shows.

35. Make funny cookies like Gingerbread men with recovering injuries.

36. Have a "Laugh-Off" to see who has the funniest, weirdest, creepiest laugh etc...

Laughter is the sun that drives winter from the human face.

-Victor Hugo

37. When out and about play "What do I do for a living?" (The game where you guess complete strangers occupations.)

38. YouTube™: David at the dentist

39. Go see improv comedy- it's also inspiring to see people think on their feet!

40. When getting your nails done pick out a funky design or color that you would NEVER normally wear!

41. Ask a child to tell you a knock-knock joke... And then let them tell it to you over and over and over again. ('Cause you know they will.)

42. Visit the website www.funnyordie.com (Author's note: if you can't find anything on here that makes you laugh- you are beyond help- just give up now move to a mountain top and call it a day.)

43. Rent, buy or download the movie: "Best in Show"

Laughter Exercise

Write down 5 of your favorite lines or scenes from the movie "Best in Show":

1.______________________________

2.______________________________

3.______________________________

4.______________________________

5.______________________________

If you can laugh at it, you can get through it.

-Karith Foster

44. Look through your high school year book- preferably with someone who will require an explanation for why your hair looks the way it does.

45. Read the morning funnies.

46. Go to a live sporting event just for the half-time/7th inning stretch games, contests and best of all- the kissing cam!

47. Do a charity 5k walk or run with people you know. Not only is it for a good cause; so many funny and good stories come out when you're doing this.

48. Check out any show about animals especially animal families- but steer clear of the ones where they eat each other (unless you find that amusing- you sick, sick person!)

49. Have friends over to play video games. Just seeing the avatar version of you is good for a laugh.

50. Go to a theme parade. Better yet be in one!

You can't stay mad at somebody who makes you laugh.

- Jay Leno

51. Play BINGO with old people- you'll be amazed & quite amused by how dead serious they take it. Octogenarians do not play when rolls of pennies and honor is on the line.

52. Try to lick your elbow.

53. Rent, buy or download a season from *Frasier*, *Everybody Loves Raymond* or *King of Queens*. Then watch it!

Laughter Exercise

Write down 5 of your favorite episodes or lines from *Frasier, Everybody Loves Raymond* or *King of Queens*:

1.____________________________

2.____________________________

3.____________________________

4.____________________________

5.____________________________

54. Youtube™: Cute Puppy Lealah "The Bra Snatcher"

55. Find one of your favorite comedian's on-line. Odds are they have clips of their comedy on their website. I believe www.karith.com has some good stuff.

56. Stay until the end of a movie just to watch the blooper reel.

Laughter is a tranquilizer with no side effects.

-Arnold Glasow

57. Have a staring contest- just like when we were kids. See who's the 1st to break a straight face.

58. Watch the *I Love Lucy* grape stomping episode then Youtube™: news anchor stomping grapes.

59. Pick up any Gary Larson "From the Far Side" book.

60. Think about the funniest commercial you've ever seen.

Laughter Exercise

Write down 5 of your favorite funny commercials:

1.______________________________

2.______________________________

3.______________________________

4.______________________________

5.______________________________

61. Go line dancing at a Country & Western bar OR more fun- a gay bar on Country & Western night.

62. Watch a roast of somebody famous.

We don't stop laughing because we grow old; we grow old because we stop laughing

-Michael Pritchard

63. Go to a charity event for animals where pets are allowed to come too.

Style
Cesar
canine cuisine
Animal Fair
www.dearlucky.com
Cesar
canine cuisine
Animal Fair
www.dearlucky.com
Cesar
canine cuisine
Animal Fair
www.dearlucky.com

64. Listen to the comedy channel on Sirius/XM

65. Remember that "one size fits all" is good in theory- but go to any state fair to witness what a false premise that is. While you're there check out ALL of the foods that apparently can be fried and consumed. Who knew?!

66. Read a humorous blog there are tons out there. (I hear www.karith.com writes about funny stuff)

67. When no one is looking make funny faces at yourself in the mirror- I promise it won't get stuck. (Or will it?)

68. Sit in at a children's play or puppet show a) to hear kids laugh (super contagious) and b) to laugh at how silly the stuff kids laugh at is.

69. Play skeeball and a game or two of air hockey with your BFF.

Children always know when company is in the living room - they can hear their mother laughing at their father's jokes

-Unknown

70. Watch old family videos.

71. Get a fake tattoo (especially if you don't have any) but let everyone who knows you think it's real.

72. Blow bubbles and have a contest with either the liquid kind or with bubble gum!

73. Visit a petting zoo. Feeding animals that essentially have no manners or etiquette is a hoot!

74. Rent, buy or download the movie "The Hangover".

Laughter Exercise

Write down 5 of your favorite lines or scenes from the movie "The Hangover":

1.____________________________

2.____________________________

3.____________________________

4.____________________________

5.____________________________

76. YouTube™: Paco & Ramsey

77. Have people over for dinner.

Time spent laughing is time spent with the gods.

-Japanese Proverb

78. Go to a comedy club during the week to see the aspiring comics try to get in the game. (Sometimes it's so bad it's good!)

79. Visit a pet store. (If it won't depress you.)

80. Go to Chuck E. Cheese again or for the first time. (And try not to look creepy- there are children there!)

81. Watch a "corny" scary movie. Nothing gets you cracking up more than laughing at yourself or someone else who gets freaked out.

Laughter Exercise

List 5 of your all-time favorite "corny" scary movies:

1.____________________________

2.____________________________

3.____________________________

4.____________________________

5.____________________________

82. Get yourself to a trivia game night at a bar, pub or coffee shop.

83. If you're not into the Super Bowl, Animal Planet airs a show at the same time called *Puppy Bowl*. Yes, it's exactly what it sounds like. Puppies on a "football field"- chasing a ball and tackling one another. They even have puppy-cams for their viewpoint & a water bowl cam so you can see them having a "timeout".

At the height of laughter, the universe is flung into a kaleidoscope of new possibilities.

-Jean Houston

84. Next time you're at a party or a club and the music is really good- start the "Soul Train" line dance. See how many moves you remember from high school.

85. Have a joke contest with your co-workers.

86. Watch the *I Love Lucy* "Vitameatavegamin" episode and the Carol Burnett's "Went With the Wind" sketch. They're both classics!

87. See if you can get a group of people to sing the opening song for one of the following classic shows: *The Love Boat, Diff'rent Strokes, Three's Company, The Jeffersons, Facts of Life* or *Good Times.*

88. Rent, buy or download a season from the sitcoms *Cheers, The Cosby Show* or *Night Court*.

Laughter Exercise

Write down 5 of your favorite episodes or lines from *Cheers*, *The Cosby Show* or *Night Court*:

1.______________________________

2.______________________________

3.______________________________

4.______________________________

5.______________________________

89. Go to a sports bar & cheer for the opposing team but have a good reason you're backing them so you don't get your you-know-what kicked.

90. Watch fireworks live somewhere! Nothing makes me more giddy! I start laughing at myself for being such a kid. If it doesn't have the same effect for you then watch someone like me...the giddiness is contagious.

91. Play with a kitten. (But beware, as they don't have full control of their claws yet. Don't get mad if you get scratched!)

92. Rent, buy or download a Mel Brooks movie: "Blazing Saddles", "Young Frankenstein", or "Spaceballs" are GREAT choices.

Laughter Exercise

Write down 5 of your favorite lines or scenes from a Mel Brooks movie:

1. ______________________________

2. ______________________________

3. ______________________________

4. ______________________________

5. ______________________________

93. Sing Karaoke... (enough said).

94. Have a face-making contest with a kid.

95. Visit the website www.overheardinnewyork.com *Bonus: If you have the opportunity, walk down the streets of NYC and keep your ears open so that you can contribute to the hilarity.

96. Think about your most embarrassing moment.

Laughter Exercise

That's right! Write out your most embarrassing moment. (Doing this will take the sting off):

____

____

____

____

____

97. You must check out the website:

www.peopleofwalmart.com

(My family is on there too!)

98. Write down the top 5 funniest movies you've ever seen. Then rent, buy or download them to watch over a rainy weekend.

Laughter Exercise

List 5 of your all-time favorite funny movies:

1.________________________

2.________________________

3.________________________

4.________________________

5.________________________

99. Watch old game shows like the *Newlywed Game, Password* or *Hollywood Squares.*

100. Attend a story telling event- where regular people like you & me get up & tell real stories from their lives. Better yet participate in a story telling event.

101. Read this book over & over again and implement the ideas I've given you because I love you and I want you to have a life filled with joy and LOTS of laughter.

Notes:

Funny Things I've Seen:

Notes:

Funny Things I've Overheard:

Notes:

Funny Things I've Done:

About the Author

Karith Foster is a successful stand-up comedian, motivational speaker, TV & radio personality, actress, author and entrepreneur. Karith is CEO and Founder of Laughter Bootcamp™ a personal development workshop which she conducts for small groups, organizations and corporations. Learn more at www.laughterbootcamp.com and be sure to check out www.karith.com

Karith is resides in both New York City and Los Angeles.